BEARPORT BIOGRAPHIES

PRESIDENT JOE BIDEN

AMERICA'S 46TH PRESIDENT

by Rachel Rose

Consultant: Heather Stockinger, Educator

BEARPORT
PUBLISHING

Minneapolis, Minnesota

Credits

Cover and Title page, Andrew Cutraro, White House photographer/Public Domain; 4, © Eva Marie Uzcategui Trinkl/Anadolu Agency via Getty Images; 5, Carolyn Cole/Los Angeles Times via Getty Images; 6, © Christopher Seliga/Wikimedia; 7, © Office of United States Senator Joe Biden/Wikimedia; 8, © gregobagel/iStock Photo; 9, © POOL/REUTERS/Newscom; 10, © Bettmann/Getty Images; 11, © Joseph Biden Office/Newscom; 12, © Bettmann/Getty Images; 13, © Bettmann/Getty Images; 14, © Office of United States Senator Joe Biden/Wikimedia; 15, © Cynthia Johnson/Getty Images; 16, © Olivier Douliery-Pool/Getty Images; 17, © Bloomberg/Getty Images; 18, © Mark Wilson/Getty Images; 19, © Pool/Getty Images; 20, © Sarah Silbiger/Bloomberg via Getty Images; 21, © Robert Deutsch/USA Today/Bloomberg via Getty Images; 22T, © Bettmann/Getty Images; 22M, © Cynthia Johnson/Getty Images; 22B, © Olivier Douliery-Pool

President: Jen Jenson
Director of Product Development: Spencer Brinker
Editor: Allison Juda
Photo Research: Book Buddy Media

Library of Congress Cataloging-in-Publication Data

Names: Rose, Rachel, 1968– author.
Title: President Joe Biden : America's 46th president / Rachel Rose.
Other titles: America's 46th president
Description: Minneapolis, Minnesota : Bearport Publishing Company, [2021] |
   Series: Bearport biographies | Ttitle from cover. | Includes
   bibliographical references and index.
Identifiers: LCCN 2020042947 (print) | LCCN 2020042948 (ebook) | ISBN
   9781647477219 (library binding) | ISBN 9781647477295 (paperback) | ISBN
   9781647477370 (ebook)
Subjects: LCSH: Biden, Joseph R., Jr. | Presidents—United States—Juvenile
   literature. | Politicians—United States—Biography. | Presidential
   candidates—United States—Biography. | United States—Politics and
   government—2017- | Legislators—United States—Biography. | United
   States. Congress. Senate—Biography. | United States—Politics and
   government—1945-1989. | United States—Politics and government—1989- |
   Delaware—Biography.
Classification: LCC E840.8.B54 R67 2021 (print) | LCC E840.8.B54 (ebook)
   | DDC 973.932092 [B]—dc23
LC record available at https://lccn.loc.gov/2020042947
LC ebook record available at https://lccn.loc.gov/2020042948

For more information, write to Bearport Publishing, 5357 Penn Avenue South, Minneapolis, MN 55419.
Printed in the United States of America.

Contents

The Next President

Joe Biden jogged onto the stage as the crowd cheered and clapped. The United States had voted, and the results were in. After days of counting, it was announced that Joe would be the country's next president. Joe spoke to the crowd. He promised to help build a stronger nation.

Joe's fans across the country cheer as he takes the stage.

Joe won the most votes for president in United States history. A record 75 million people voted for him.

Hardworking Joe

Joseph Robinette Biden Jr. was born in Scranton, Pennsylvania, on November 20, 1942. When he was young, Joe stood out because he had a **stutter**. Other children at school made fun of him. Joe's parents taught him to stand up to bullies. They told him that being different didn't mean he couldn't do great things. Joe took this advice to heart.

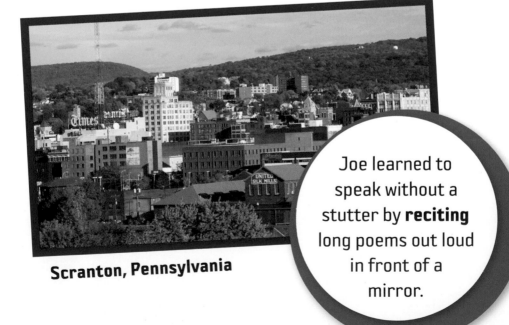

Scranton, Pennsylvania

Joe learned to speak without a stutter by **reciting** long poems out loud in front of a mirror.

When Joe was 10, his family moved to Claymont, Delaware. A few years later, he started going to Archmere Academy, a **private** Catholic school. It cost a lot of money to go to Archmere, so Joe washed windows and picked weeds there to help his parents pay for school. Then, Joe went on to study history, **political science**, and law.

Joe went to the University of Delaware from 1961 to 1965.

Joe played football at Archmere Academy and in college. His Archmere coach said Joe was a great player.

Politics and Heartbreak

Joe married his college sweetheart, Neilia Hunter, in 1966. They started a family, and Joe became a lawyer. Soon, he also entered **politics**. He served on the local **county council** before being elected to the U.S. Senate in 1972. In December of that year, tragedy struck. Joe's wife and baby daughter were killed in a car accident. His two sons were badly hurt.

Joe celebrates his 30th birthday with his family

Joe had just turned 30 when he became a senator, making him one of the youngest senators in history.

Joe with his sons, Hunter *(left)* and Beau *(right)*, in the summer of 1972

Joe was heartbroken over the death of his wife and baby. But he did his best to take on his new job as senator and look after his two young boys. While most senators live in Washington, D.C., Joe stayed at home in Delaware so he could be with his sons. That meant he traveled 120 miles (190 km) to go to work in Washington every day!

Joe took his **oath** to become senator from his son Beau's hospital room.

Joe traveling to work in 1973

White House Dreams

As a senator, Joe became an expert in **foreign policy**. He did well in his role and would serve in the Senate for 36 years. But he had big dreams that went beyond the Senate. In 1987, Joe ran for president, but he dropped out of the race early. He tried again in 2007, but he was no match for Hillary Clinton and Barack Obama.

Joe and Jill

Joe found love again. In 1977, he married Jill Jacobs.

Joe during his first run for president

Still, Joe's hopes for the White House were not over yet. When Barack was **nominated** for president, he picked Joe to run as his vice president. In 2008, they were elected to become the country's top leaders. Joe's main role was to help the president with foreign policy and the **economy**. Joe and Barack worked well together. Soon, they became close friends.

Joe and Barack talk at the White House

Joe joined Barack every morning to talk about what was happening in the country. They often met multiple times a day.

Barack and Joe celebrate their win in 2008

In 2012, Barack and Joe were reelected. They would serve four more years as president and vice president. Joe worked hard on issues such as stopping gun **violence**, creating more jobs, and supporting energy that does not harm the **environment**. Barack wanted to show the world how much Joe had done for the country. He gave Joe the Presidential Medal of Freedom.

Beau Biden

Joe's son Beau died of brain cancer in 2015. This inspired Joe to lead an effort to find a cure for cancer.

Barack surprised Joe
with the Presidential
Medal of Freedom.

Third Time's the Charm

After his job as vice president was over, Joe continued to work hard and fight for what he believed in. But it wasn't long before he was back in the same place he had been twice before. In 2019, Joe decided to run for president. In 2020, he won!

Kamala Harris

Joe's vice president, Kamala Harris, is the first woman in the country to be elected to that position.

Timeline

Here are some key dates in Joe Biden's life.

1940
Born on
November 20

1972
Loses his wife
and baby in a car
accident

1973
Becomes
a senator

1977
Marries for the
second time

1987
Runs for
president for
the first time

2009
Becomes vice
president

2017
Is given the
Presidential Medal
of Freedom

2020
Is elected
president

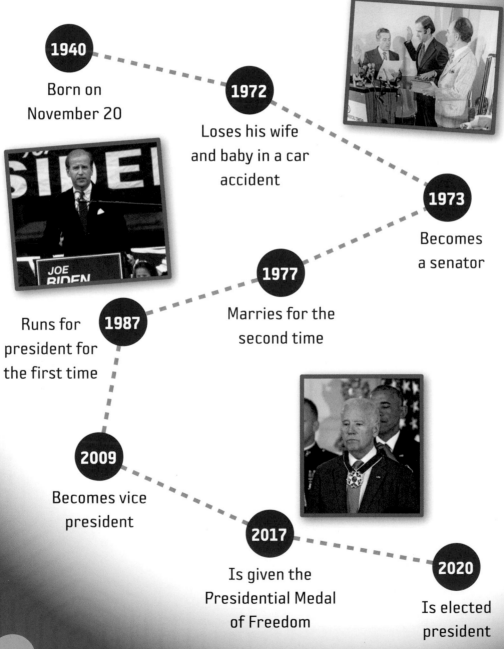

Glossary

county council an elected group of people who manage a county

economy the way in which goods and services are made, sold, and used in a country

environment the area where an animal or plant lives and all the things, such as weather, that affect that place

foreign policy a government's way of interacting with other nations

nominated chosen as a person to run in an election

oath a serious promise; in politics, people take an oath to follow the law and do their jobs fairly and justly

political science the study of government

politics the activities, actions, and plans that are used to gain and hold power in a government

private schools that are not run by the state or government

reciting repeating something from memory

stutter a way of speaking when parts of words are repeated

violence harmful force

Index

Read More

Collison, Campbell. *The Presidents (X-Treme Facts: U.S. History).* Minneapolis: Bearport Publishing, 2021.

Harts, Shannon H. *Voting for the President of the United States (U.S. Presidential Elections: How They Work).* New York: PowerKids Press, 2020.

Learn More Online

1. Go to **www.factsurfer.com**
2. Enter "**Joe Biden**" into the search box.
3. Click on the cover of this book to see a list of websites.

About the Author

Rachel Rose is a writer who lives in San Francisco. Her favorite books to write are about people who lead inspiring lives.